THE LION KING

MUSIC FROM THE MOTION PICTURE SOUNDTRACK

ISBN 978-1-5400-6753-1

Motion Picture Artwork TM & Copyright © 2019 Disney

HAL•LEONARD®

Visit Hal Leonard Online at
www.halleonard.com

Contact us:
Hal Leonard
7777 West Bluemound Road
Milwaukee, WI 53213
Email: info@halleonard.com

In Europe, contact:
Hal Leonard Europe Limited
42 Wigmore Street
Marylebone, London, W1U 2RN
Email: info@halleonardeurope.com

In Australia, contact:
Hal Leonard Australia Pty. Ltd.
4 Lentara Court
Cheltenham, Victoria, 3192 Australia
Email: info@halleonard.com.au

CONTENTS

Can You Feel The Love Tonight

Music by ELTON JOHN
Lyrics by TIM RICE

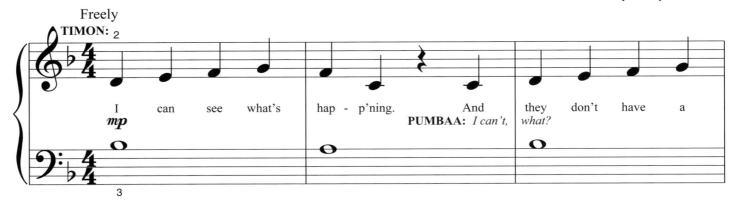

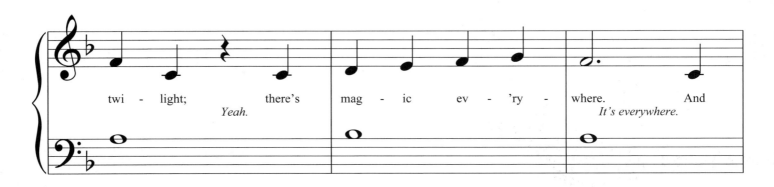

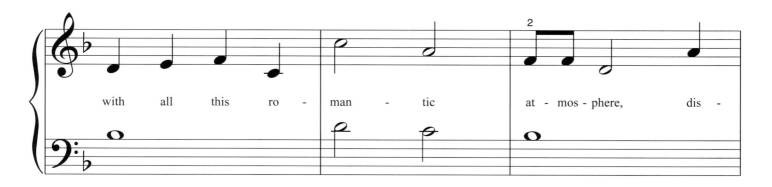

with all this ro - man - tic at - mos - phere, dis -

Moderately

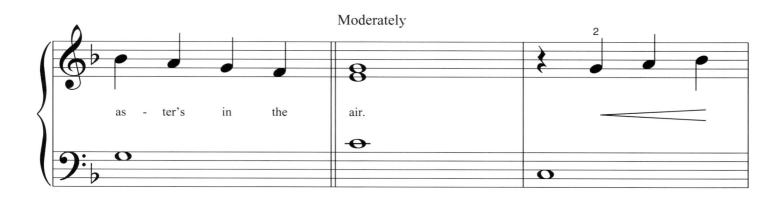

as - ter's in the air.

NALA & SIMBA:

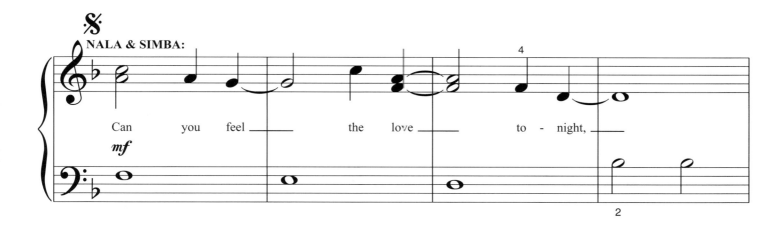

Can you feel ____ the love ____ to - night, ____

mf

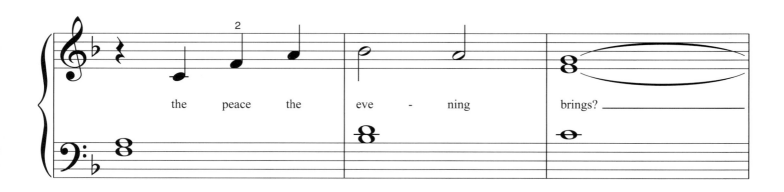

the peace the eve - ning brings? ____

The world, for once, in

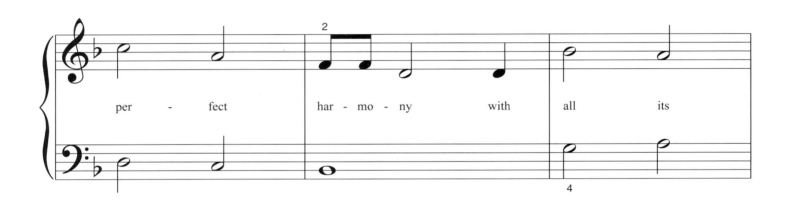

per - fect har - mo - ny with all its

To Coda ⊕

SIMBA:

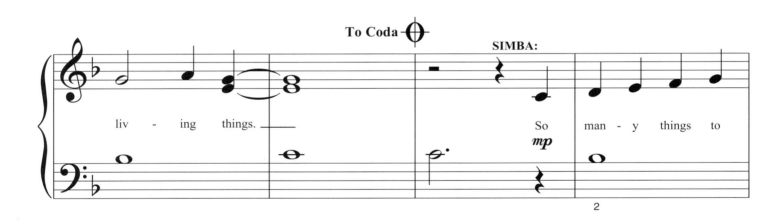

liv - ing things. So man - y things to

mp

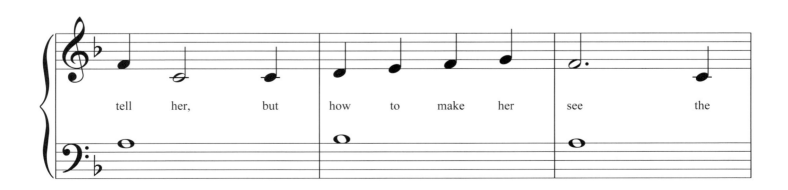

tell her, but how to make her see the

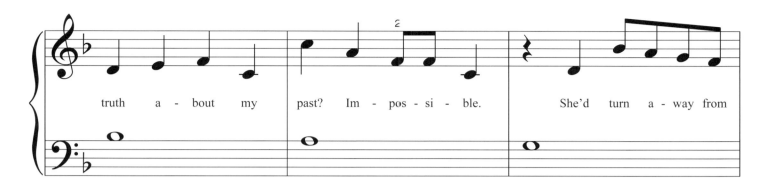

truth a - bout my past? Im - pos - si - ble. She'd turn a - way from

NALA:

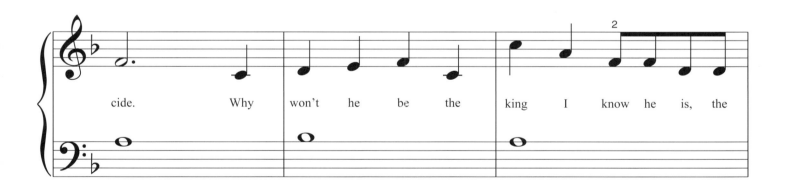

me. He's hold - ing back, he's hid - ing. But what? I can't de -

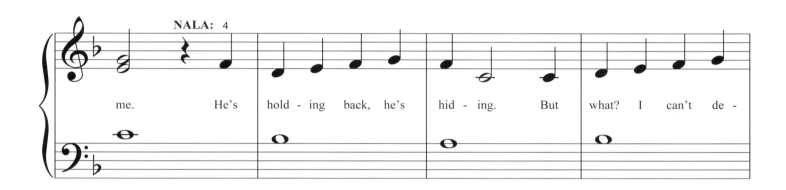

cide. Why won't he be the king I know he is, the

D.S. al Coda

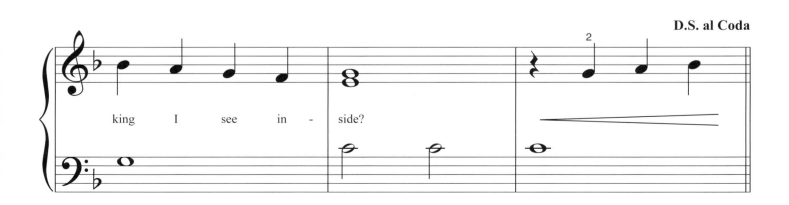

king I see in - side?

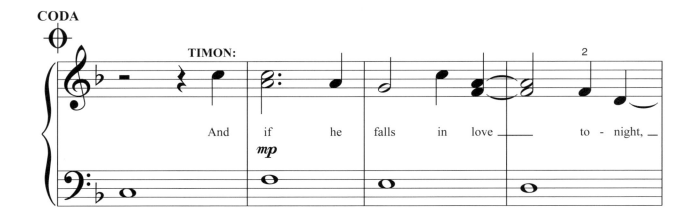

CODA

TIMON:

And if he falls in love to - night,

mp

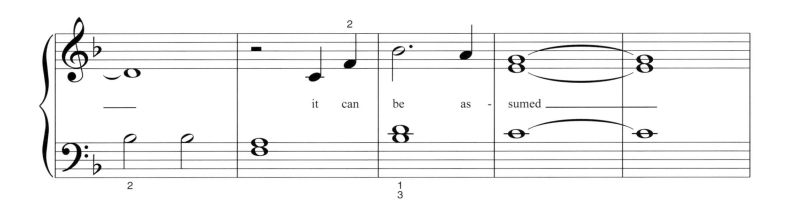

it can be as - sumed

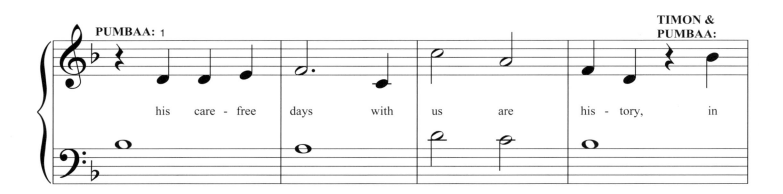

PUMBAA:

TIMON &
PUMBAA:

his care - free days with us are his - tory, in

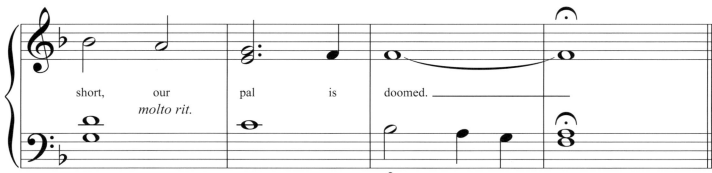

short, our pal is doomed.

molto rit.

2

CIRCLE OF LIFE/
NANTS' INGONYAMA

Moderately

NANTS' INGONYAMA
Music and Lyrics by HANS ZIMMER and LEBOHANG MORAKE

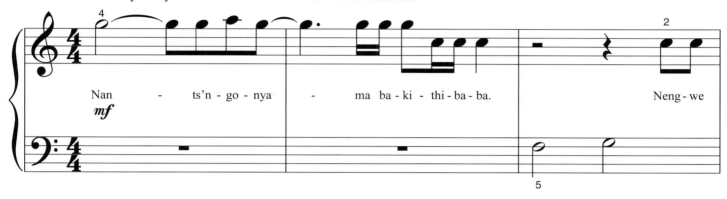

Nan - ts'n - go - nya - ma ba - ki - thi - ba - ba. Neng - we

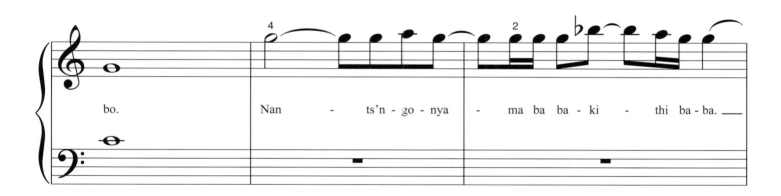

bo. Nan - ts'n - go - nya - ma ba ba - ki - thi ba - ba.

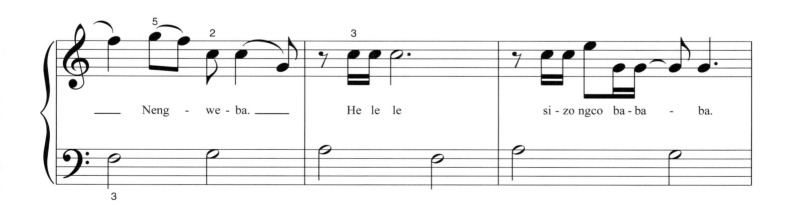

Neng - we - ba. He le le si - zo ngco ba - ba - ba.

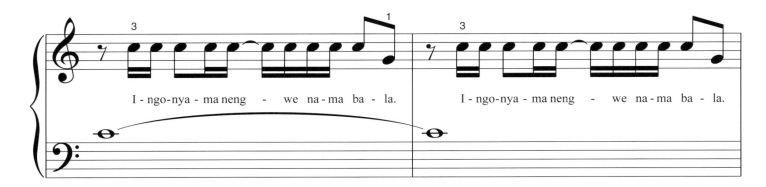

I - ngo-nya - ma neng - we na-ma ba - la.   I - ngo-nya - ma neng - we na-ma ba - la.

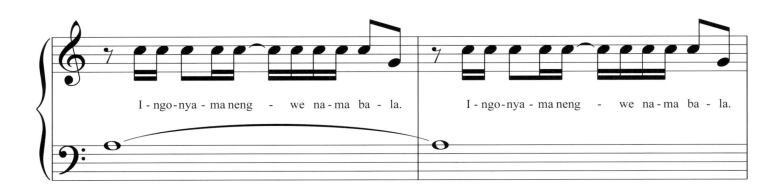

I - ngo-nya - ma neng - we na-ma ba - la.   I - ngo-nya - ma neng - we na-ma ba - la.

I - ngo-nya - ma neng - we na-ma ba - la.   I - ngo-nya - ma neng - we na-ma ba - la.

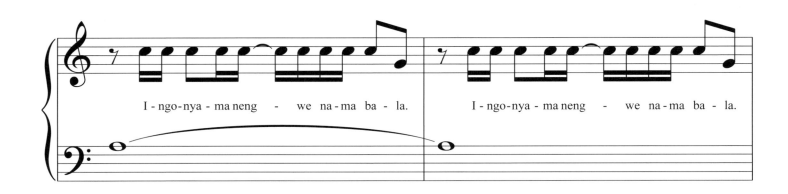

I - ngo-nya - ma neng - we na-ma ba - la.   I - ngo-nya - ma neng - we na-ma ba - la.

CIRCLE OF LIFE
Music by ELTON JOHN
Lyrics by TIM RICE

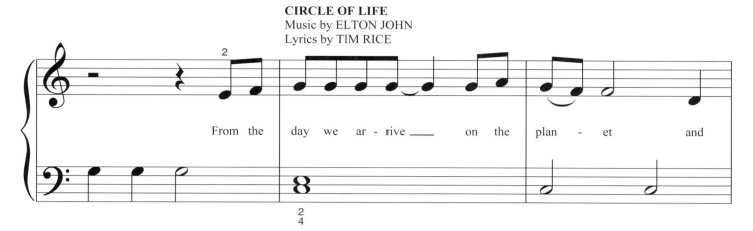

From the day we ar - rive ____ on the plan - et and

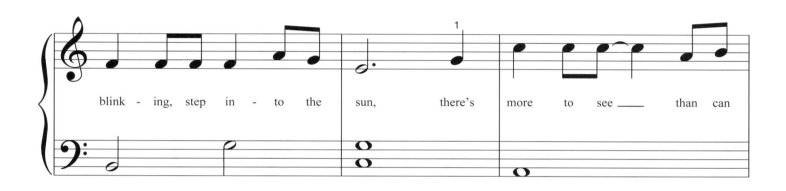

blink - ing, step in - to the sun, there's more to see ____ than can

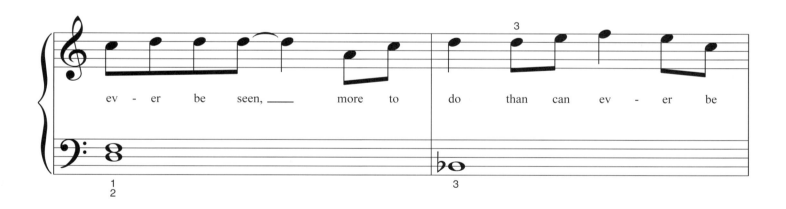

ev - er be seen, ____ more to do than can ev - er be

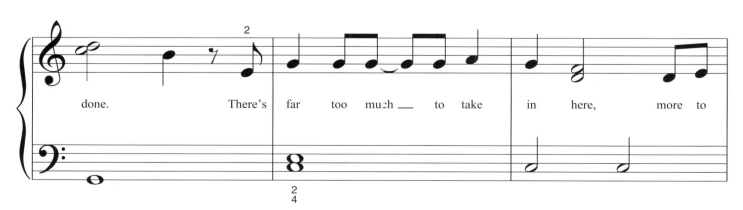

done. There's far too much ____ to take in here, more to

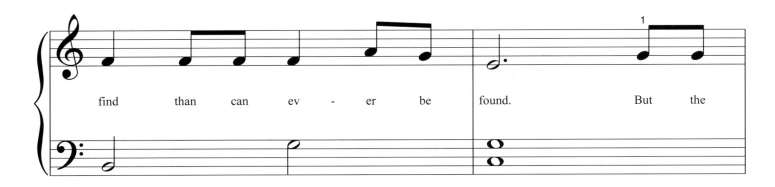

find than can ev - er be found. But the

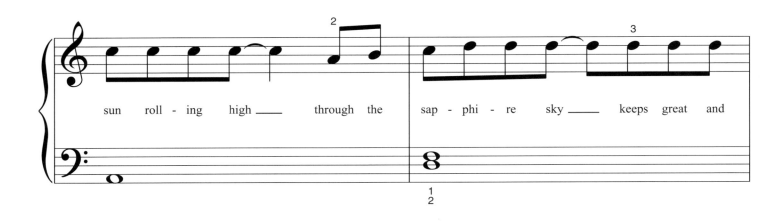

sun roll - ing high ____ through the sap - phi - re sky ____ keeps great and

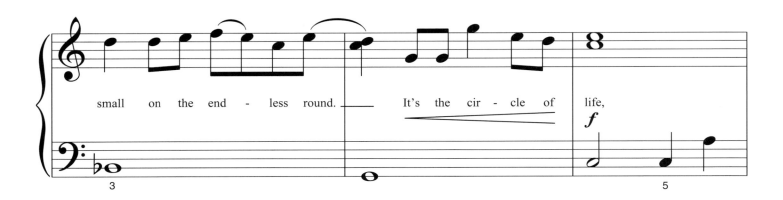

small on the end - less round. ____ It's the cir - cle of life,

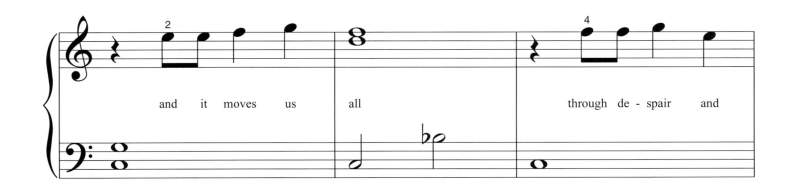

and it moves us all through de - spair and

hope, _____ through faith and _____ love,

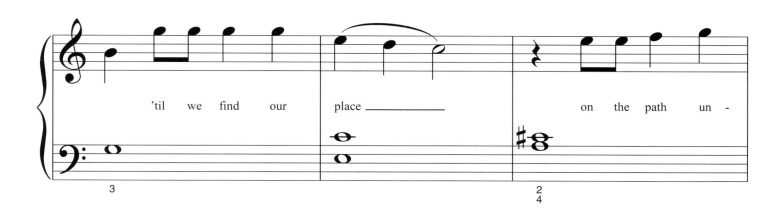

'til we find our place _____ on the path un -

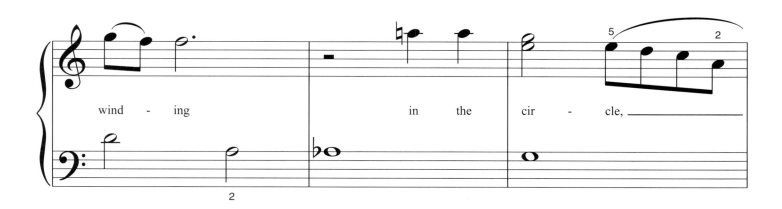

wind - ing in the cir - cle, _____

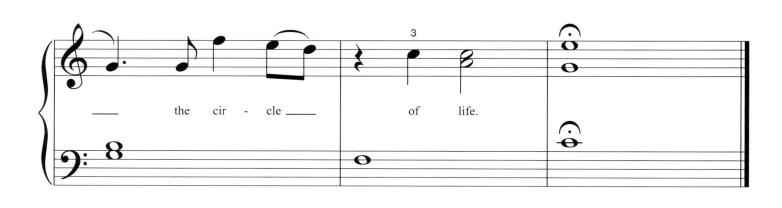

_____ the cir - cle _____ of life.

HAKUNA MATATA

Music by ELTON JOHN
Lyrics by TIM RICE

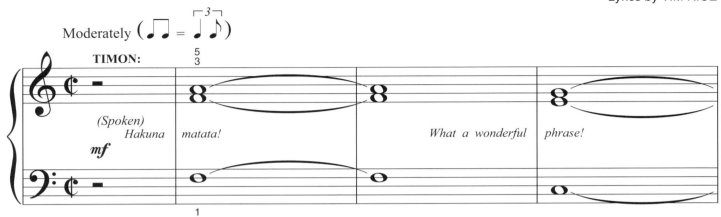

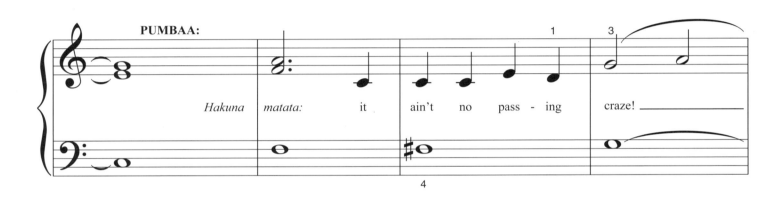

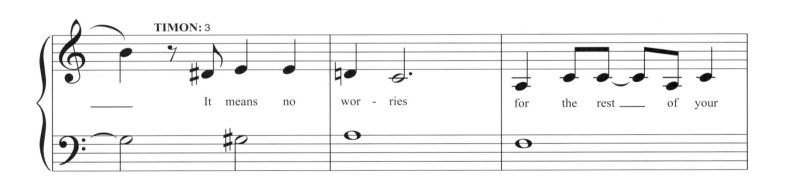

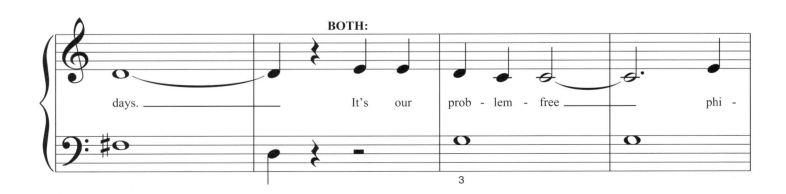

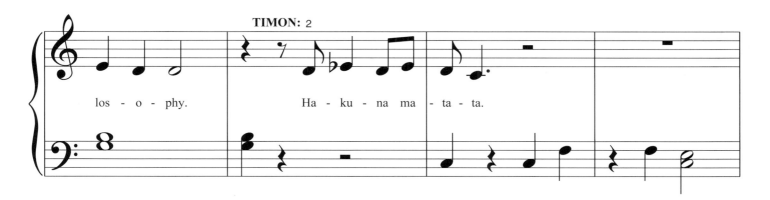

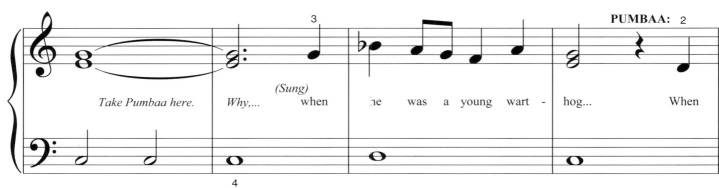

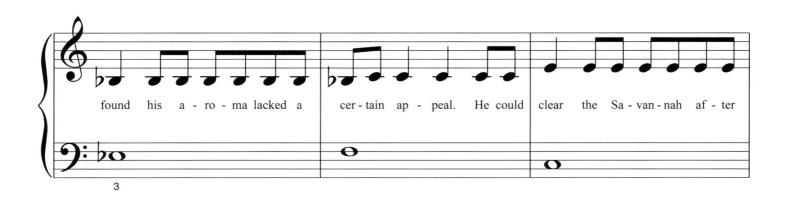

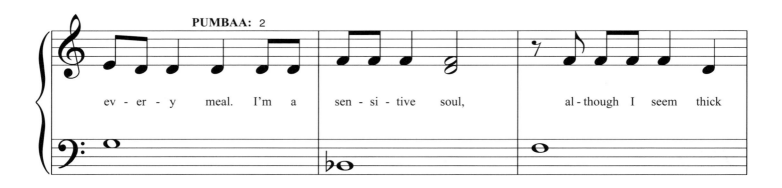

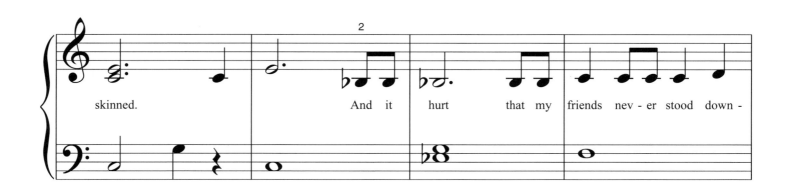

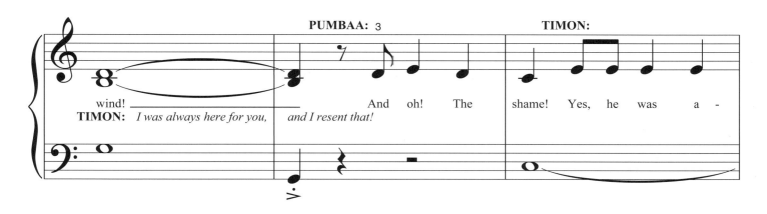

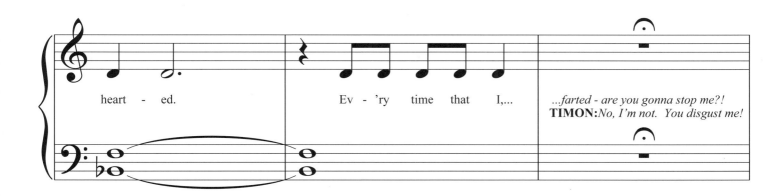

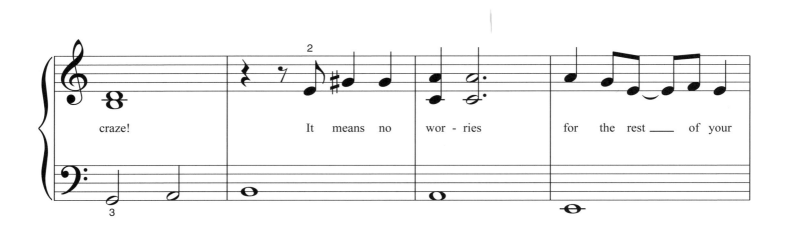

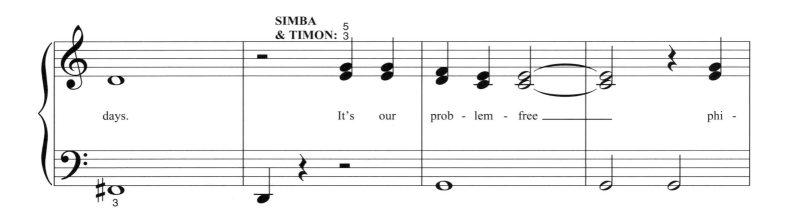

HE LIVES IN YOU

Music and Lyrics by MARK MANCINA,
JAY RIFKIN and LEBOHANG MORAKE

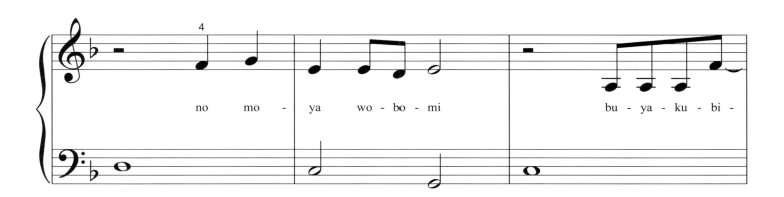

Ne - zwi. _____ E - li no -

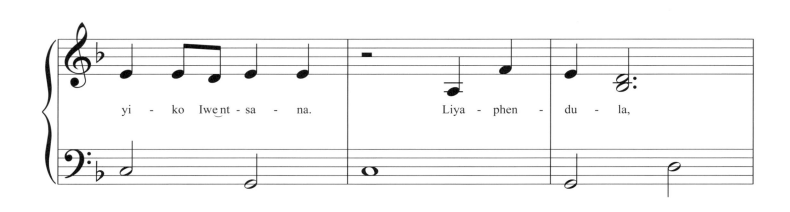

yi - ko Iwent-sa - na. Liya-phen - du - la,

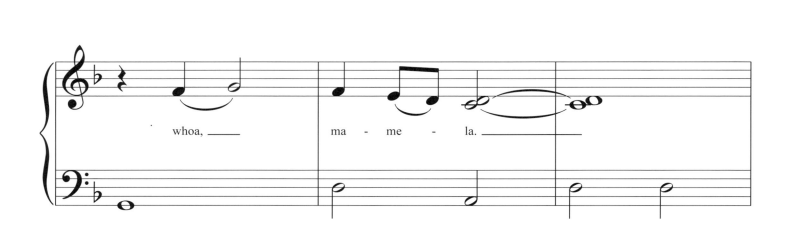

whoa, _____ ma - me - la. _____

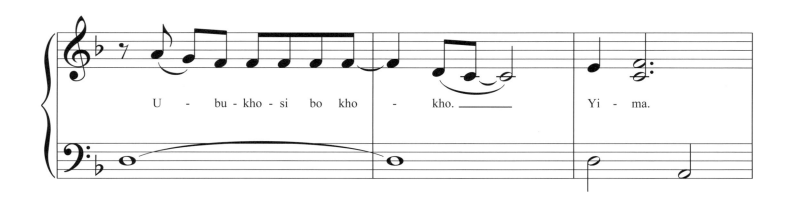

U - bu-kho-si bo kho - kho. _____ Yi - ma.

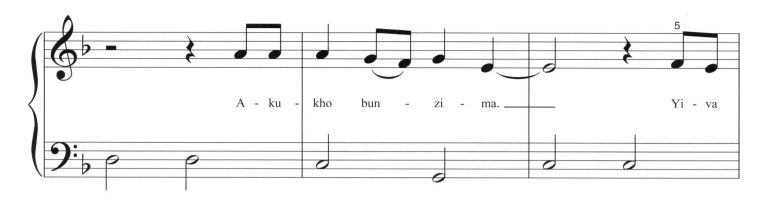

A - ku - kho bun – zi - ma. Yi - va

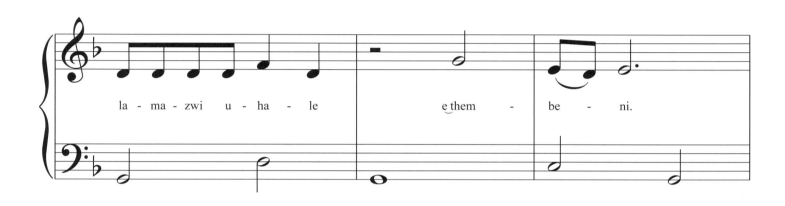

la - ma - zwi u - ha - le e them – be – ni.

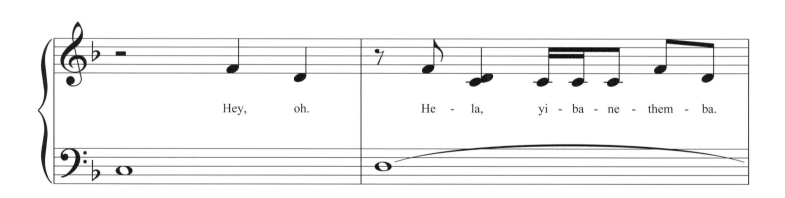

Hey, oh. He - la, yi - ba - ne - them - ba.

He - la, yi - ba - ne - them - ba He - la, yi - ba - ne - them - ba.

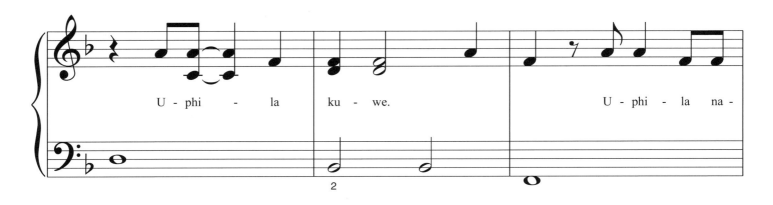

U - phi - la - ku - we. U - phi - la na -

kum. U - hla - l'e - jon - gi - le.

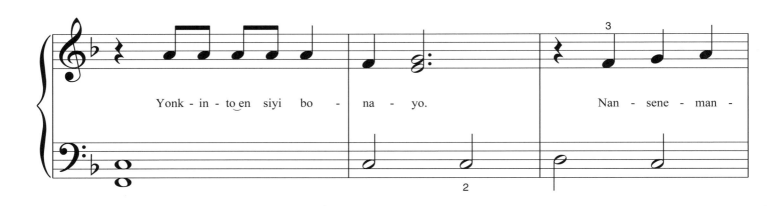

Yonk - in - to en siyi bo - na - yo. Nan - sene - man -

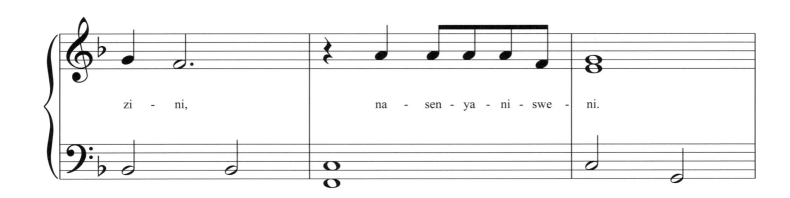

zi - ni, na - sen - ya - ni - swe - ni.

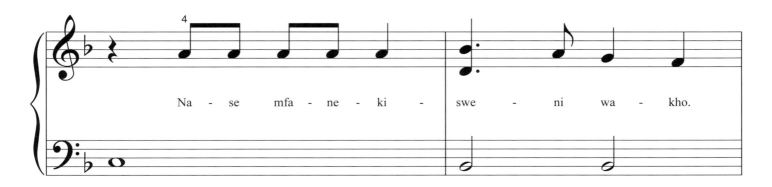

Na - se mfa - ne - ki - swe - ni wa - kho.

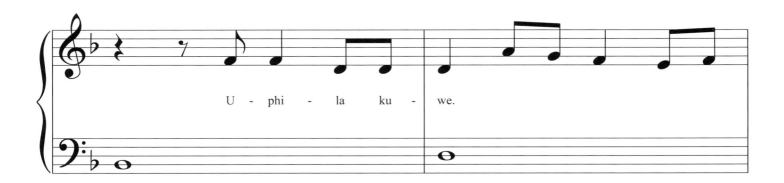

U - phi - la ku - we.

English Translation

Here is a lion and a striped tiger.
Night and the spirit of life, calling. Listen.
And a voice, with the fear of a child, answers. Listen.
Throne of the ancestors.
Wait. There's no mountain too great.
Hear these words and have faith. Have faith.
Hey, listen.
He lives in you. He lives in me.
He watches over everything we see.
Into the water, into the truth,
In your reflection, he lives in you.
He lives in you.

I JUST CAN'T WAIT TO BE KING

Music by ELTON JOHN
Lyrics by TIM RICE

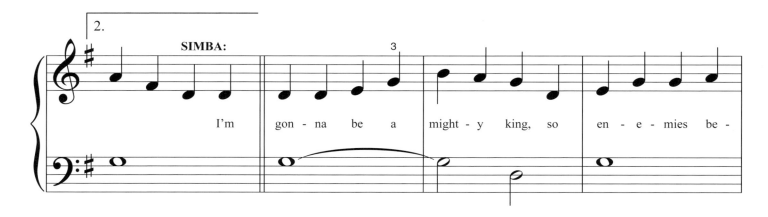

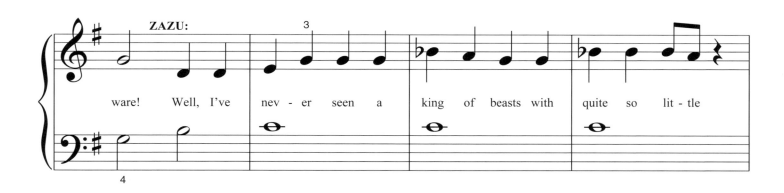

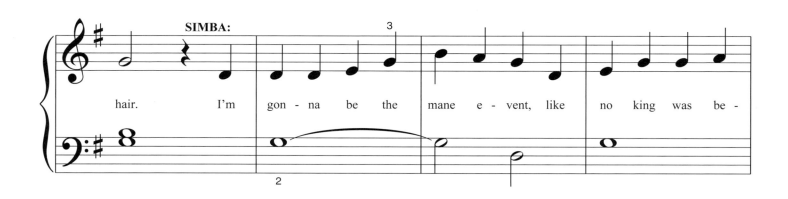

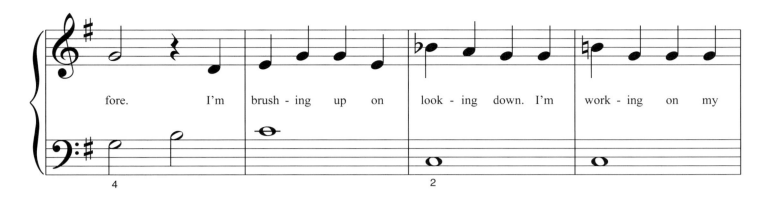

fore.　I'm　brush - ing　up　on　look - ing　down. I'm　work - ing　on　my

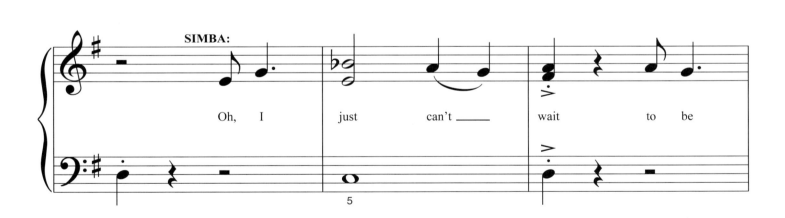

ZAZU:

roar!　Thus　far,　a　rath - er　un - in - spir - ing　thing.

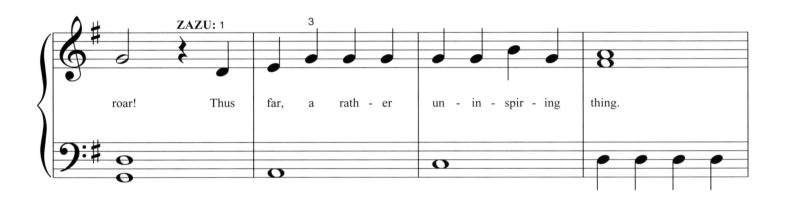

SIMBA:

Oh,　I　just　can't ____　wait　to　be

king!　　　　　　I　think　it's　time　that

26

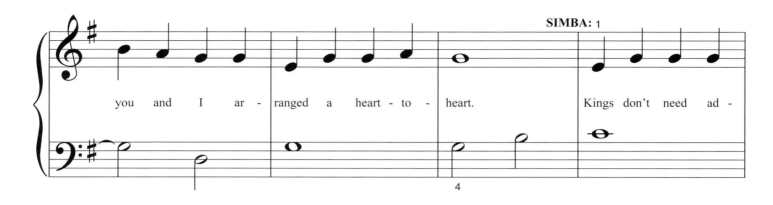

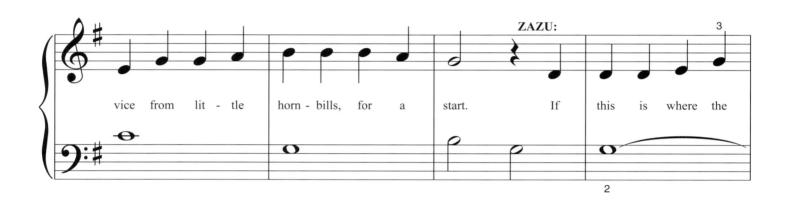

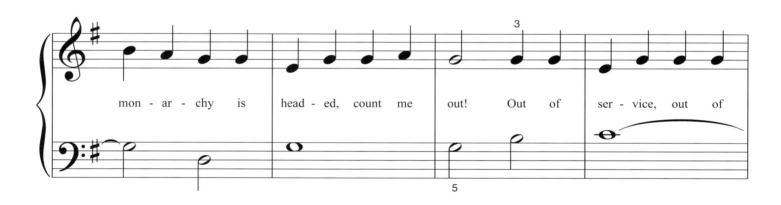

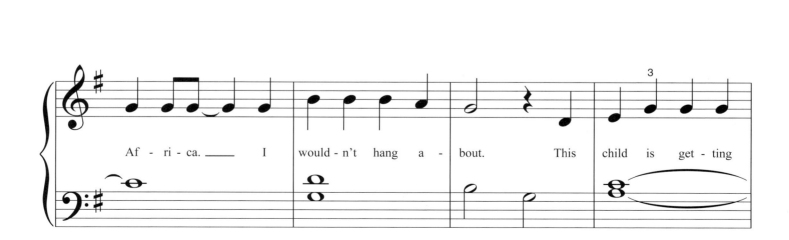

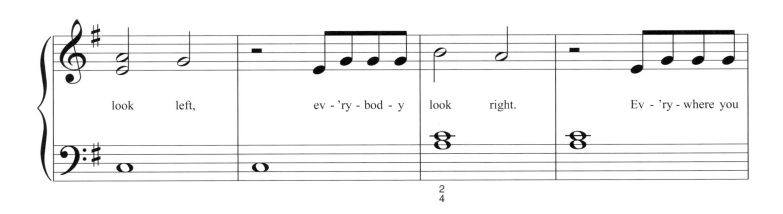

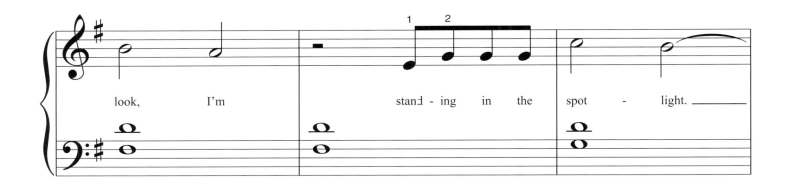

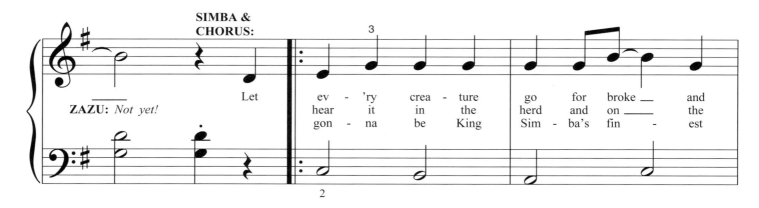

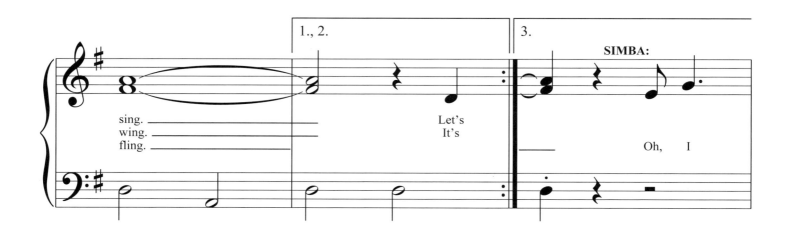

SPIRIT

Written by TIMOTHY McKENZIE,
ILYA SALMANZADEH and BEYONCÉ

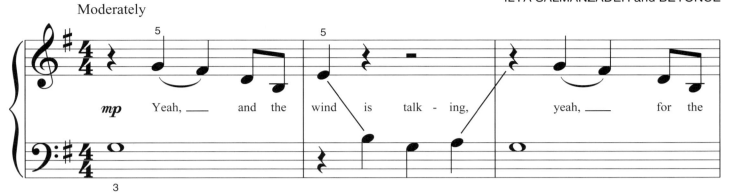

Yeah, ____ and the wind is talk - ing, yeah, ____ for the

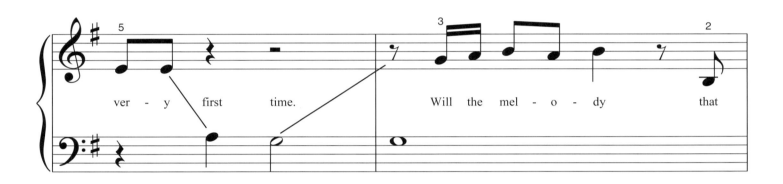

ver - y first time. Will the mel - o - dy that

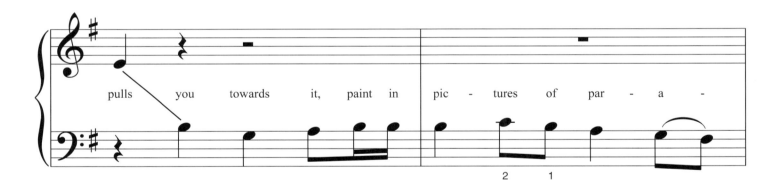

pulls you towards it, paint in pic - tures of par - a -

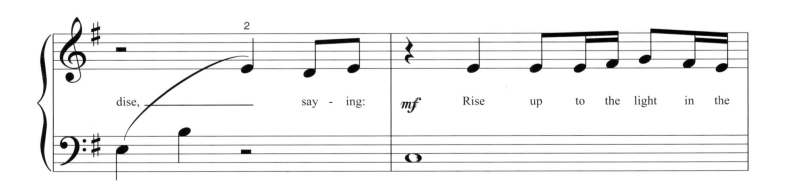

dise, ____ say - ing: Rise up to the light in the

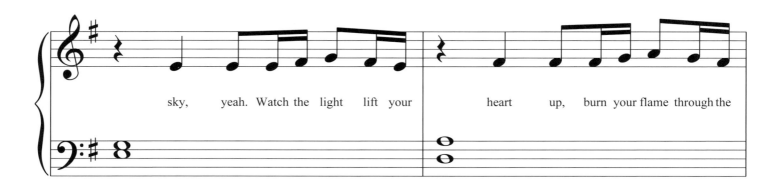

sky,   yeah. Watch the light   lift your   heart   up,   burn your flame through the

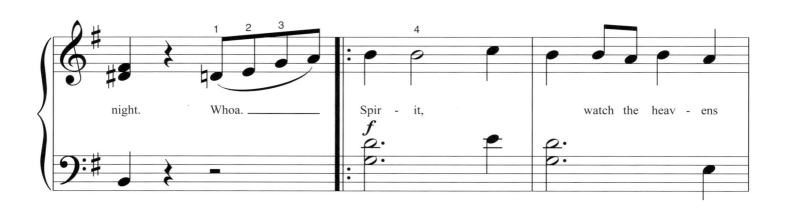

night.   Whoa.   Spir - it,   watch the heav - ens

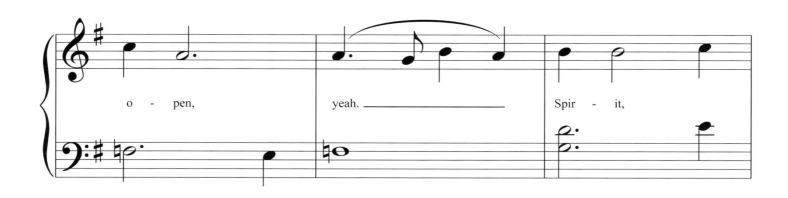

o - pen,   yeah.   Spir - it,

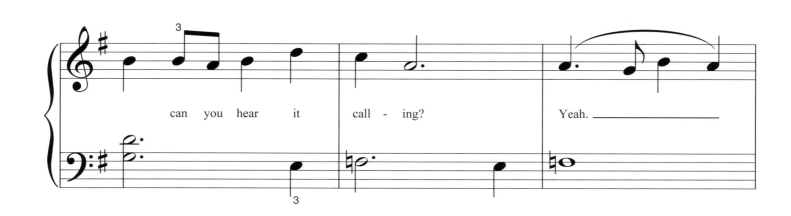

can you hear it call - ing?   Yeah.

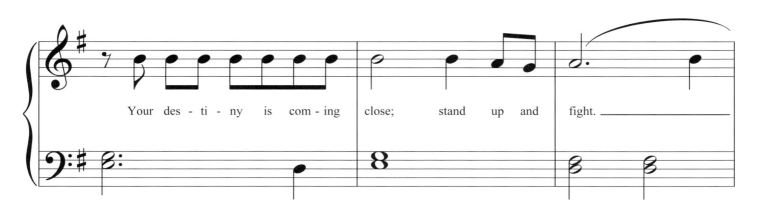

Your des - ti - ny is com - ing close; stand up and fight. _____

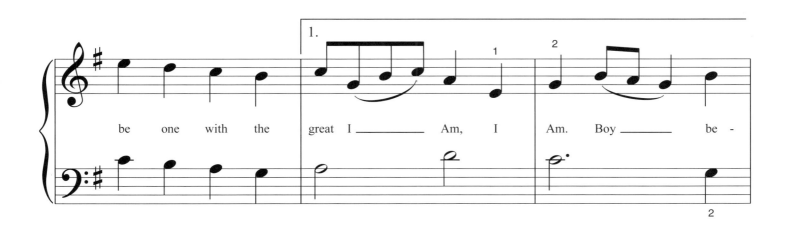

_____ So, go in - to that far ___ off ___ land and

mp

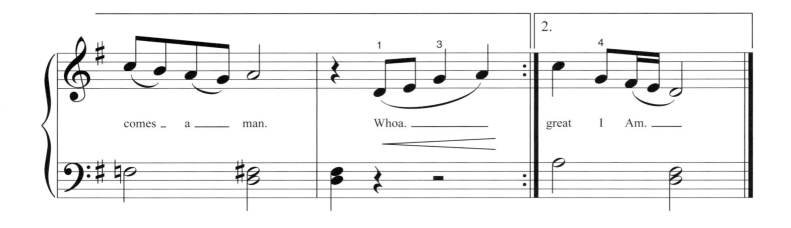

be one with the great I _____ Am, I Am. Boy _____ be -

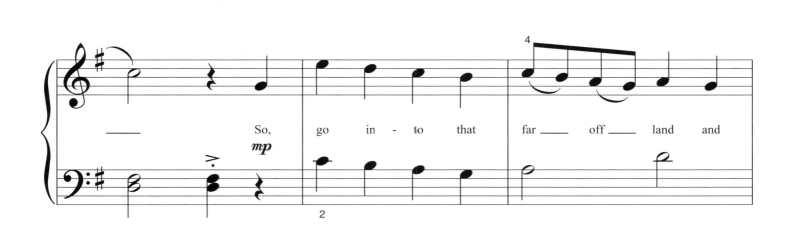

comes _ a ___ man. Whoa. _____ great I Am. _____

THE LION SLEEPS TONIGHT

New Lyrics and Revised Music by GEORGE DAVID WEISS,
HUGO PERETTI and LUIGI CREATORE

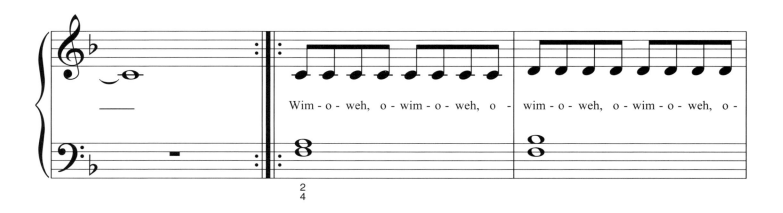

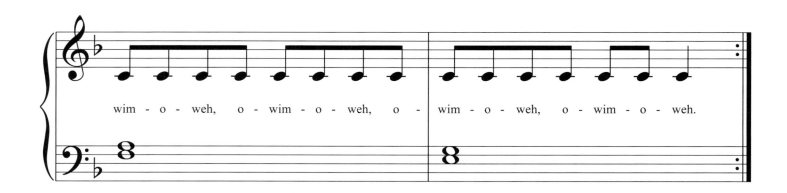

In the jun - gle, the might - y jun - gle, the
Near the vil - lage, the peace - ful vil - lage, the
Hush, my dar - ling, don't fear, my dar - ling, the

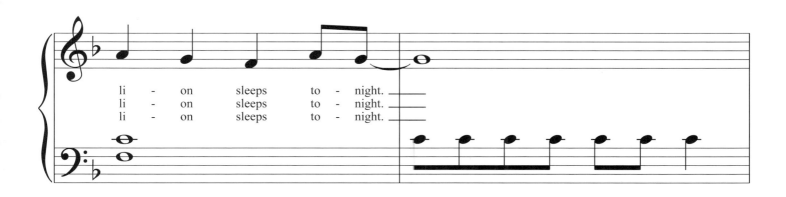

li - on sleeps to - night.
li - on sleeps to - night.
li - on sleeps to - night.

In the jun - gle, the might - y jun - gle, the
Near the vil - lage, the qui - et vil - lage, the
Hush, my dar - ling, don't fear, my dar - ling, the

To Coda ⊕

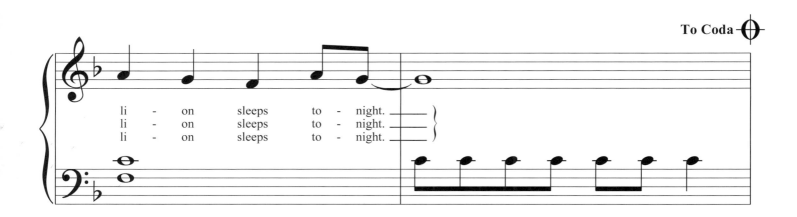

li - on sleeps to - night.
li - on sleeps to - night.
li - on sleeps to - night.

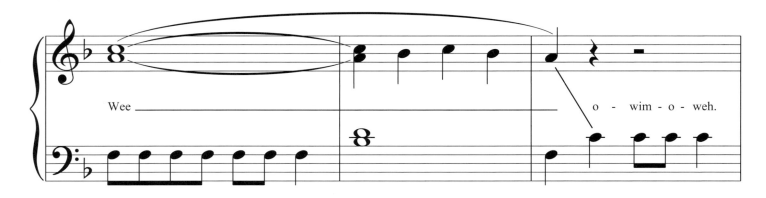

Wee _____ o - wim - o - weh.

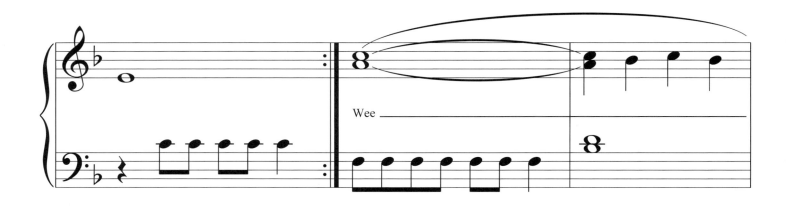

Wee _____

_____ o - wim - o - weh.

8va

D.S. al Coda

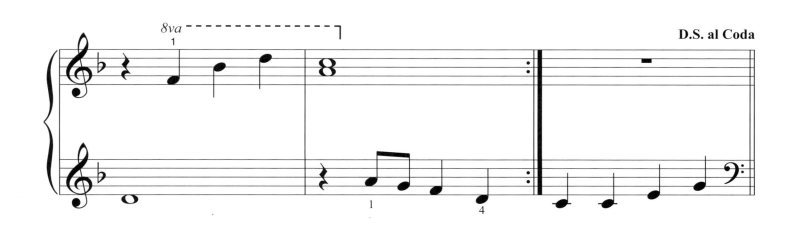

CODA

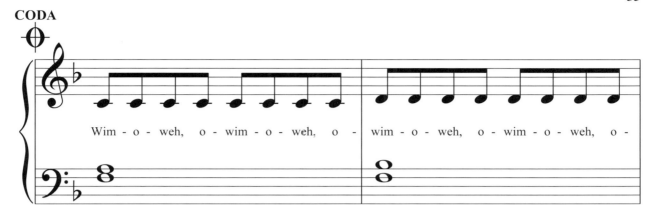

Wim - o - weh, o - wim - o - weh, o - wim - o - weh, o - wim - o - weh, o -

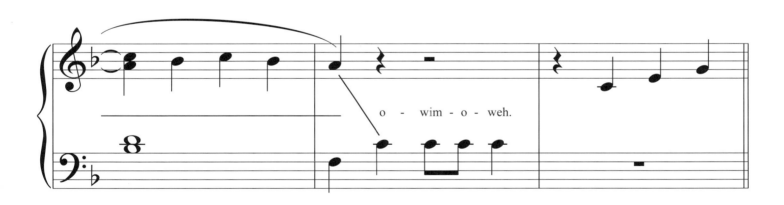

wim - o - weh, o - wim - o - weh, o - wim - o - weh, o - wim - o - weh.   Wee _____

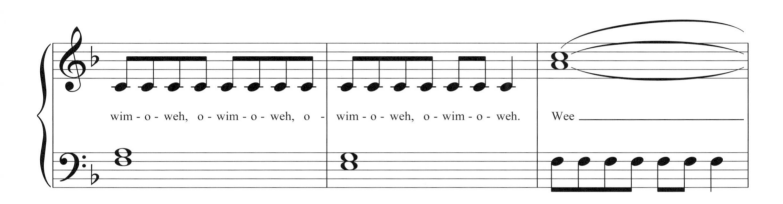

o - wim - o - weh.

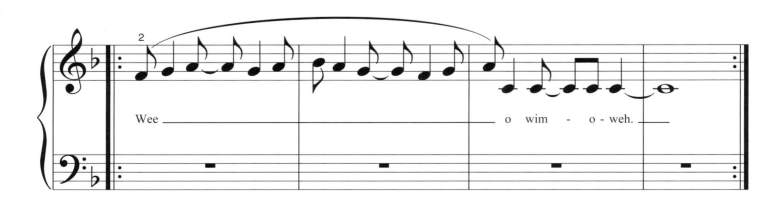

Wee _____   o - wim - o - weh. _____

NEVER TOO LATE

Music by ELTON JOHN
Lyrics by TIM RICE

Moderately fast

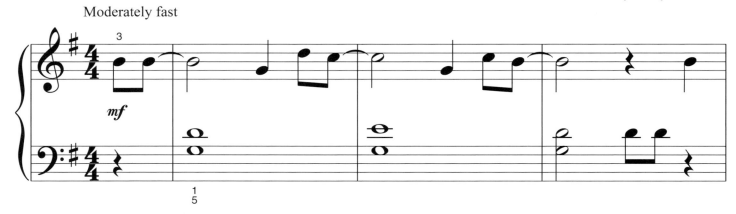

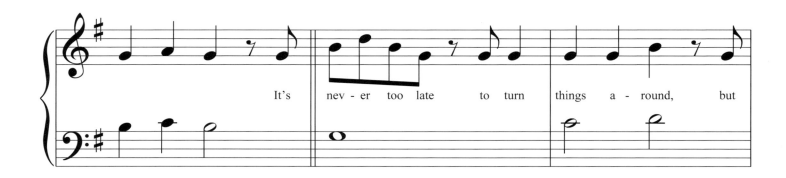

It's nev-er too late to turn things a-round, but

come and un-rav - el the path ___ to con - found. The

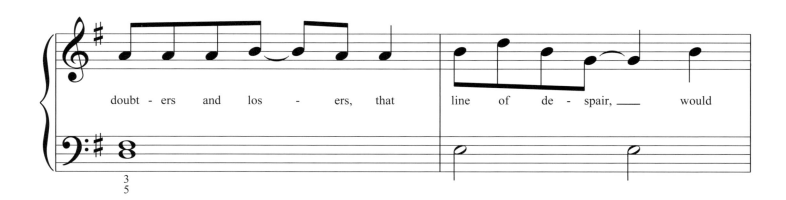

doubt-ers and los - ers, that line of de-spair, ___ would

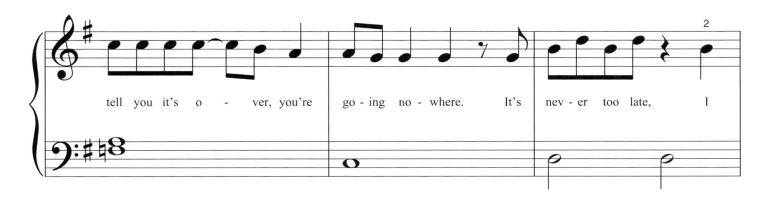

tell you it's o - ver, you're go - ing no - where. It's nev - er too late, I

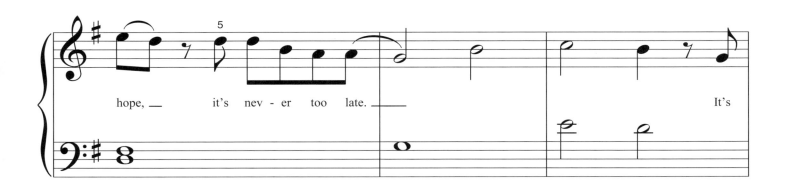

hope, ___ it's nev - er too late. ___ It's

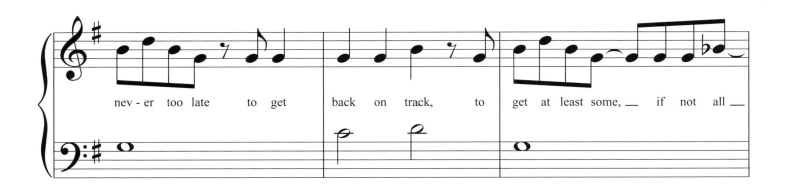

nev - er too late to get back on track, to get at least some, ___ if not all ___

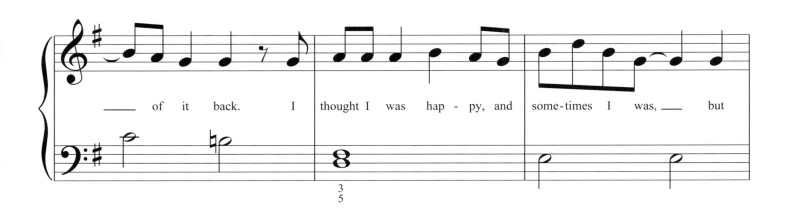

___ of it back. I thought I was hap - py, and some - times I was, ___ but

38

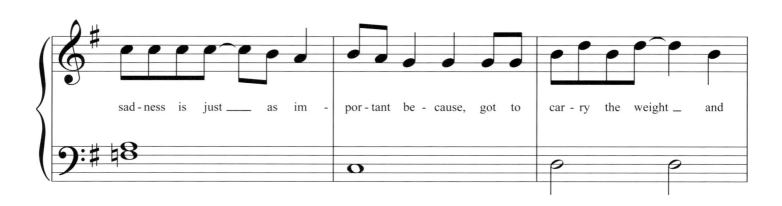

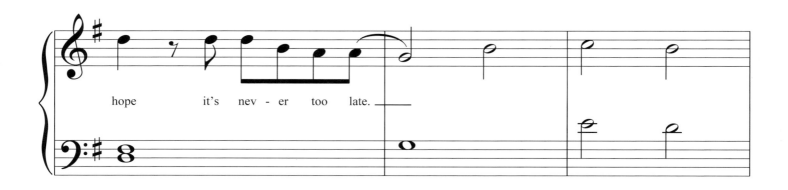

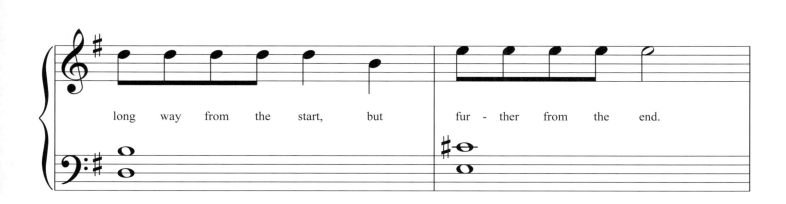

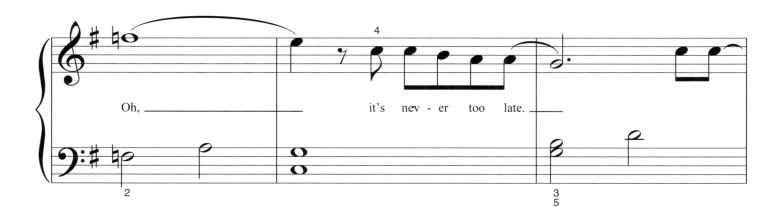